THE LITTLE
BOOK OF
LANCASHIRE

edited by Alan Crosby

First published in Great Britain 2005 by Dalesman
an imprint of
Country Publications Ltd
The Water Mill, Broughton Hall
Skipton, North Yorkshire BD23 3AG

Text selection © Alan Crosby 2005

ISBN 185568 222 2

Printed for Compass Press Ltd

Introduction

Once there was a county universally regarded by outsiders as cold, wet, poor and backward, where depressing terraced houses huddled on grimy streets against a backdrop of bleak, gloomy moors, where the people were barely civilised and spoke an incomprehensible dialect. Well, Yorkshire is like that to this day. This book, on the other hand, is about Lancashire, whose beautiful hills provide the backdrop to fascinating towns, whose seaside is noted for fresh air and fun, and whose friendly, generous people welcome visitors. Read on and discover quotations old and new, comments from outsiders (some fair-minded, some hostile and therefore wrong) and samples of Lancashire's wealth of humour. You'll see why nobody in their right mind could doubt that, north of the Mersey and south of the Lake District, west of the Pennines and east of the Irish Sea, lies a land which is truly blessed.

A resort which has been variously described as 'an earthly paradise' and 'the only place which doesn't remind you of somewhere else'.

Robert Hayes' Guide to Blackpool, *1928*

At Blackpool, where something like
a cool million has been spent in
providing gorgeous palaces of
pleasure, the nimble sixpence will
buy ten times more entertainment
than it will at Brighton, Margate or
any other places frequented by
Londoners of the working class.

F Ormerod, Lancashire Life
and Character, *1915*

An old man … attended the village festival and was accosted by the vicar, who said: 'You are an old man. What is your age?' 'Well,' said the man, 'my mother says I am eighty-two.' 'You mean your mother told you,' said the vicar. 'No, she told me the other day I was eighty-two'. Said the incredulous vicar, 'Why, what age is she if you are eighty-two?'. 'She's a hundred and three', said the son, proudly.

F Ormerod, about St Michael's on Wyre

All you that come to read this Stone
Consider how soon I was gone
Death Sometimes do no warning give
Therefore be Carefull how you live

tombstone of 1806,
Goodshaw Chapel, Rossendale

There's gradely hounds in Lancashire,
as such there always were;
There's gradely hills in Lancashire,
as how they're bleak and bare
There's jannock lads in Lancashire,
and that I wish yo true
An' I wish't I was in Lancashire,
all the day through.

Cicely Fox Smith
(jannock = strong, honest, reliable)

'Young uns cawn't heyt eat these days,' said John Tommy, spreading some sausage on his bread with the communal knife. 'Aw remembers takkin' eighteen slices fo' mi breakfast and dinner, an' theer's bin nowt left fo' mi dinner.'

John Tommy of Bacup, from Herbert Collins, The Roof of Lancashire, *1950*

As soon as ever we entered the town, we found the streets lined on both sides with multitudes of people, shouting, cursing, blaspheming, and gnashing upon us with their teeth. Perceiving it would not be practical to preach abroad, I went into a large room open to the street and called aloud, 'Let the wicked forsake his way, and the unrighteous man his thoughts' [but] we perceived the lions of Rochdale were lambs in comparison of those at Bolton.

John Wesley visiting Lancashire, 1749

In the evening I walk'd about the church yard, and in several walks, throng'd by Sunday company, naked leg'd boys, and impudent wenches, before I return'd to my supper of a black fowl, with bad bread, and one candle.

John Byng, on Rochdale, 1795

Wigan, were it not inhabited by a race of sturdy and rather tough Lancashire folk, would be the most self-conscious town in England. For years it has suffered from a joke … Now, I had been in Wigan just ten minutes when I saw that there is no joke! 'This town has been badly libelled', I said to a man who was standing in the main street. 'I'm reet glad to hear thee say that!', he cried warmly, 'I've lived in Wigan all my life, and wish for no better town'.

H V Morton,
In Search of England, *1927*

Liverpoole is one of the
wonders of Britain.

Daniel Defoe, 1724

Preston is a fine town … full of attorneys, proctors, and notaries … The people are gay here, though not perhaps the richer for that; but it has by that obtained the name of Proud Preston.

Daniel Defoe, 1724

It was a town of red brick, or of red brick that would have been red if the smoke and ashes had allowed it, but as matters stood it was a town of unnatural red and black like the painted face of a savage.

Charles Dickens in Hard Times *about Coketown, which was Preston, 1854*

The doctor may sneer if he pleases
But my recipe never will fail
For the physic that cures all diseases
Is a bumper of Warrington ale.

I do not give an ounce of credence
to the sacrilege, perpetrated by
politicians, of bending the
boundaries to put us [Warrington] in
Cheshire. The best word I ever saw
that summed up it all was invented
by an acquaintance of mine for a
Lancashire Life competition:
LANCASTRATION.

Alan Beswick, 1991

There I entred Lancashire, the mist began to lessen, and as I descended on this side the fog more and more went off and a little rain fell, tho' at a little distance in our view the sun shone on the vale … a fruitfull valley full of inclosures and cut hedges and trees.

Celia Fiennes coming from Yorkshire, 1695

More money, more muck; more muck, more money: the only flaw in the system being that the money tended to go in an opposite direction from that of the muck.

J B Priestley, a native of Bradford, on Lancashire

As a manufacturing Town it rises superior to any in the Kingdom … The Voice of Industry is heard on every hand, Idleness is disgraceful, and a Man without Business, or some occupation, Manchester does not own. The ingenuity of her Artizans is amazing. One would suppose they had already arrived at the Summit of Invention, and had left nothing for Posterity to boast an improvement in.

Jabez Fisher, an American Quaker, 1775

The fairest, best built, quickest and most populous town in Lancashire.

John Leland on Manchester, 1536

Lancashire readers will know that when I speak of a muffin, I'm not referring to the café kind or those of south country origin, but a speciality of our own, baked on the backstone or oven bottom. There's no muffin to beat it anywhere.

J Barlow Brookes, 1947

Meight when we're hungry,
Drink when we're dry,
Brass when we're short on't,
An' heaven when we die.

old Lancashire toast

Aw'st gerrup afore th' sparrow farts

*traditional reference to rising early
in the morning*

Some folk can lie till th' clock strikes eight
Some folk may sleep till ten
Then rub their e'en an' yawn a bit
An' turn 'em o'er again;
Some folk can ring a bell i' bed
Till th' sarvant brings some tay;
But weet or dry, a factory lad
Mun jump at break o' day!

Edwin Waugh, The factory bell, *1881*

choose-heaw	anyhow, however
choose-hooa	whoever
choose-what	whatever
choose-wheer	wherever
choosen-when	whenever

F E Taylor,
from his Lancashire dictionary, 1901

Th' owd lingo talked bi gradely fooak
Th' owd lingo as eawr faythers spooak,
Th' own lingo as we hooap 'll leaven
Th' whul lot o' Babel tongues i' heaven.

Joseph Baron, on Lancashire dialect, 1890

Tommy Thumper
Cherry Bumper
Long Lacy
Billy Milker
and Little Top o' town's End

children's finger rhyme from Burnley

The church at little Winwick
It stands upon a sod
And when a maid is married there
The steeple gives a nod
Alas! How many ages
Their rapid flight have flown
Since on that high and lofty spire
There's moved a single stone.

traditional rhyme
(maid = virgin)

Be kearfu', he'll put Yorksher on thi.

*Yorkshire = a Lancashire noun meaning
a trick, cheat or deception*

'A Wonder,
or An Honest Yorkshireman'

title of 1736 ballad opera by Henry Carey

To see this grand sight, we soon got
a good place
It surpass'd all the world for
beauty and grace,
There were feathers and flounces
and bosoms like snow,
In beautiful ringlets their hair it did flow,
The ladies' procession was walking,
The noblemen laughing and talking,
While each jolly farmer was gawping,
To catch all the fun at the Guild.

A New Song on Preston Guild, 1822

One of the most dismal, dilapidated, disgraceful-looking structures in Christendom. It was not only very ill-looking but ... exceedingly inconvenient and dangerous.

Preston Railway Station,
before rebuilding in 1880

Middleton folk: moonrakers
Heywood folk: Monkey Towners
Westhoughton folk: Coo'yeds
Penwortham folk: Bunnocks

Pilling Moss, like God's Grace,
knows no bounds.

old saying

Time-honoured Lancaster

Shakespeare, Richard II

Lancashire, like lyons,
layden them aboute!

ballad about the battle of Flodden Field,
1513

In 1577, Hollinshead noted with approval and surprise that at 'the inns in Lancaster, Preston, Wigan and Warrington … each comer is sure to lie in clean sheets wherein no man hath lodged'.

One of the most Princeliest and Stateliest peeces of our Sovereigne Ladie, the Queene's, auncyent inheritance.

description of the Duchy of Lancaster in 1555

His souldiers and clubmen were glad of it, that they might eate their Christmas pyes at home.

in the Civil War, of Sir Gilbert Houghton's men when he decided not to lay siege to Blackburn, 24th December 1642

In 1827, for a wager, James Isherwood of Haslingden ate twenty raw eggs, including the shells, in seven minutes; in 1866, at the Wellington Inn in nearby Haslingden Grane, a local man gave up when his 'jaws were brought to a deadlock' after eating three-quarters of a 4lb suet pudding.

from Chris Aspin, Lancashire: The First Industrial Society, *1995*

I know not in the whole range of language terms sufficiently expressive to describe the infernal highway. Let me most seriously caution all travellers who may accidentally propose to travel this terrible country to avoid it as they would the devil.

Arthur Young, on the road from Preston to Wigan, 1770

The procession must have been the grandest ever beheld, whether we consider the triumph of mechanical art which it exhibited … or the brilliant display of rank and talent, beauty and fashion, which it contained.

the opening of the Liverpool and Manchester Railway, 1830

I have observed that in the manners and deportment of the people of the lower orders in Lancashire there is at all times something peculiar and very far from prepossessing. A stranger would unquestionably pronounce them rude, coarse and insolent.

Richard Ayton, 1813

Drunkenness is so prevalent that I doubt whether it would be possible to travel half a dozen miles in any public road in Lancashire without seeing some indication of it.

Joseph Livesey, founder of the Temperance movement, 1831

We Blackpoolers always like to come to Lytham because it's such a well-laid-out town, which is not surprising as it's been such a long time dead.

quoted by John Kennedy, 1990

One circumstance must above all others render Lytham dear to those who have a strict regard to morality — vice has not erected her standard here. The numerous tribes of professional gamblers, unhappy profligates and fashionable swindlers find employment and rapine elsewhere.

Peter Whittle, 1799

Four for a penny,
Eh! What a many,
Ripe and ready,
Mellow yellow pears

street cry of a fruitseller
in Manchester, 1850s

48

Passed thro' Ormskirk, famous for its gingerbread, which is certainly very good.

Anne Borrodaile, 1831

If His Majesty of Great Britain would grant him pardon and leave to live the rest of his days in Lancashire … he should deem himself one of the happiest in the world.

the exiled Catholic leader, Cardinal William Allen, writing in the reign of James I

All Lancashire for the most part
The lusty Stanley stout can lead
A stock of striplings strong of heart
Brought up from babes with beef
and bread.

ballad on Flodden Field, 1513

The city always looks as if it had
been built to withstand foul weather.

J B Priestley on Manchester, 1934

Nowhere else can the life and conditions of the industrial proletariat be studied in all their aspects as in South Lancashire. Here can be seen the degradation into which the worker sinks.

Friedrich Engels, 1844

A lonely tract of high, rounded fells broken by gritstone crags and limestone knolls; golden streams rushing down secluded valleys; lonely farmsteads set in networks of drystone walls; and quiet villages among lush meadows; these are the qualities of the Forest of Bowland.

AA Discovering Britain *guide, 1982*

A quiet, dignified, rather
opulent town.

*Peter Fleetwood-Hesketh, 1970,
on Southport*

A common drunkard, and such an
ale knight as the like is not in our
parish … he will, when he cannot
discern black from blue, dance
with a full cup on his head.

*a late sixteenth-century vicar of Whalley,
brought before the Bishop of Chester*

Eggs I want and money I crave,
If you don't give me eggs
I'll sweep you all to your grave.

pace-egging chant at Poulton-le-Fylde,
eighteenth century

Thence to Garstang, pray you hark it
Ent'ring there a great beast market
As I jogged on to the street
'Twas my fortune, for to meet
A young heifer who before her
Took me up and threw me o'er her.

Richard Braithwaite's greeting
in Garstang, 1638

The neighbourhood of Liverpool abounds with beautiful situations, and the villages of Everton, Kirkdale, and Bootle ... Wavertree, Toxteth Park and Allerton ... all have their appropriate beauties.

Baines, 1825

Upon the arrival of a crisp and golden apple pie, I was instructed: 'Take some of that Lancashire cheese with it: apple pie without cheese is like a kiss without a squeeze'.

John Kennedy, 1990

Lancashire cheese is an English cow's milk cheese … and perhaps the finest English cheese of all for cooking. It has a mild flavour and at about three months old is as soft as butter and can be spread like it.

Theodora FitzGibbon, 1984

Lancashire is famed far and wide
for good cooking.

Nell Heaton, 1951

A rare food pleasure I remember from the war years was walking along Morecambe Bay with my sister, each of us with a brown paper bag of shrimps. They were small and brown, the best kind. We chewed without bothering to peel all of them.

Jane Grigson, 1984

The hotpot is always served from the dish it is cooked in, and traditionally in Lancashire, pickled red cabbage is served as a side dish. It is a simple good dish, containing all the essence of the meats and vegetables. It is far superior to the French 'pot-au-feu'.

Theodora FitzGibbon, 1965

Gravy and potatoes
in a good brown pot,
Bake it in the oven
and serve it very hot.

Oldham's gift to an ever-grateful nation: it was the place where 'fish and chips' was invented.

Nelson: the only town in England named after a public house.

He attended the parish church where, if the sermon went on longer than he would ideally have liked, he used to take five shilling-pieces from his pocket and line them up in full view of the minister in front of him as his offering ... At regular intervals, however, as the service dragged on, the coins would disappear back into his pocket, providing the minister with a powerful incentive to draw to a close.

Augustus Wykeham Clifton, 1850s

A man ut thinks hissel th' first
Englishman i' th' land, but
conno talk English.

*Ben Brierley's definition
of a Cockney, 1881*

A great abuse in this Towne by reason of Carryon, dead Swyne, Doggs and other noysome, filthie carryon being throwne in St John's Weende and other back lanes.

Preston's refuse problems, 1655

England's bread hangs by
Lancashire's thread.

a jannocke of Lancashyre

*part of the shepherds' feast in the Chester
mystery plays, circa 1400
('jannock' here refers to a type of thick and
substantial oatcake traditional in Lancashire)*

A tackler lived in Clitheroe, and his wife was out of sorts so she went to see the doctor. 'Take plenty of barley water', he said. She told her husband what the doctor had prescribed, and the next day the tackler set out with two buckets and brought them back full of water from Barley near Pendle.

(tackler = overlooker in cotton mill, renowned for lack of intellect)

We are the two Darren Mashers
We often go out on the Mash
We wear no tall hats or no shirts
To our backs
And seldom we have any cash.
We oftimes bring out the new fashion
And seldom stick to the old
Although we are just twenty-seven
We're handsome, stout-hearted and bold.

local song popular in Darwen, early 1930s

Between two hills, both bleak and barren,
Lies dirty little Darwen.

unjust rhyme, probably made by
Blackburners, late nineteenth century

The Queen, Duke of Lancaster

the Lancashire loyal toast

… this brawl today,
Grown to this faction in the
Temple Garden,
Shall send between the Red Rose
and the White,
A thousand souls to death and
deadly night.

Shakespeare, Henry VI part 1

In most cricket matches the critic endeavours to be impartial … The Lancashire and Yorkshire match is an exception. I step down from the pedestal of impartiality … If two Yorkshire batsmen make a long stand … I do my best to exert an influence of will over the field of play — some current of hate and malice calculated to cause mishap, if not death and destruction, to take place at the wicket for the benefit of my native county.

Neville Cardus, 1982

The Lancashire way of fighting, *purring*, or kicking your opponent with heavy wooden-soled clogs, covered with iron plates and studded with large nails.

The important part of any county is its people. Every time a Lancashire man opens his mouth he declares his native heath. Not even residence at Oxford or Cambridge can altogether erase the accent that other subjects of the King find so amusing.

Walter Greenwood 1935

Th'art welcome, little bonny brid,
But shoundn't ha' come just when
tha' did.
Toimes are bad.
We're short o' pobbies for eawr Joe.
But that, of course, tha' didn't know,
Did ta', lad?

Samuel Laycock, 1863
(pobbies = bread and milk)

There's no mistaking the lads and lasses of Lancashire. They dress like other people but their speech betrays them … Their utter disregard of conventionality is a striking trait in their character.

Pall Mall Gazette, *1884*

Shrewdness, homely simplicity, irony, fierce independence, an impish delight in mocking whatever is thought to be affected and pretentious.

J B Priestley on Lancashire women, 1934

If tha can si Pendle its benna rain,
If tha can't, its already raining.

Some folk say Pendle Hill wants
grandeur and sublimity, but they
themselves must be wanting in taste
... There is no hill in England like
Pendle Hill.

Harrison Ainsworth, 1845

Lord, we bean abawt to separate.
Do Tha go wi us on eur way an'
bless us aw for Christ sake, Amen.

East Lancashire benediction,
circa 1900

Th' Lord is mi Friend,
Wi 'im aw want fur nowt
He teks mi oe'rt moor
To a gud abidin' place
Beside quiet watter
An he meks mi feel fair comfortable
Mi soul is lifted up
An aw feel reet glad in 'is presence.

beginning of the Lord's Prayer in East Lancashire dialect

A woman was buying a bunch of black grapes at a fruit stall. 'They're for me husband', she said, ''e likes a few black grapes'. As the assistant was putting them into a bag, the woman had a sudden thought. ''Ave they bin sprayed with poison?' she asked. 'No, luv', was the reply, 'you'll 'ave ter buy that yerself from t' chemist'.

Nelly Carbis, 1992

A formidable lady and her small husband, from Bacup, were asked about their retirement plans. She replied: 'When one of us dies, I'm going to live in St Anne's'.

Eur Lanky dialect's rough, but straight;
    No lappin' up o' nowt;
Swift fro' th' heart to th' lips it runs,
Noan hauve a mile reaund th' fowt.
We ha' not time to waste i' words,
    We speik an' get it done;
An' Lancashire folk an' their dialect,
    Are as feyther an' son.

Allen Clarke, 1923

He wanted to know what gradely meant, an' I towd him at that were nobbut one meaning for it an' that were 'gradely'. It were a gradely word I said, an' if he couldno find it in th' dictionary it wern't a gradely dictionary.

Sam Fitton (1868-1923)

Little dinner carriers
Wi' big breawn deeshus
Toddlin' i' dozens wi'
The'r loaves an' feeshes
Crook't legs, straight legs,
Every sort 'at's made
Trottin' wi' the'r dinners
On the grand parade.

Sam Fitton, on taking dinner to the
millworkers at midday

Carl away, carl away.
Palm Sunday, Easter Day.

street sellers' cry, 1830s
(carls = baked peas)

Liftin' — on Easter Monday, men lifted women: several men would take hold of a woman, at least one per arm and one per leg, and raise her horizontally into the air, three times. On Easter Tuesday, groups of women would lift men. The objective of the exercise must remain the subject of speculation.

describing an old Lancashire custom

Races by nude men are not yet
extinct in many parts of Lancashire,
notwithstanding the vigilance of
the county police.

*John Harland, 1878 (the Rochdale area
was particularly noted for this sport)*

We agree that no players of interludes, jugglers, jesters or wandering people bring into this town any monstrous or strange beasts, or other uses rowdy or rare, to their lucre and the distress of the Queen's subjects.

Liverpool byelaw, 1560s

A town more famous for its beauty and populousness than its antiquity.

William Camden, 1586, about Liverpool

In the early nineteenth century Widnes was celebrated as a fashionable seaside resort, and the visitors feasted on eel-pies, cooked by the landlady of a local inn: the fish were caught in the Mersey.

Burnley for ready money
Mereclough never trust
You take a peep at Stiperden
And call at Kebs you must.

*packhorse jingle; Kebs was an inn
on the road to Heptonstall*

Lewd sports tending to no other end but to stir up our frail natures to wantonness with embracings, kissings and unchaste beholding of each other and marching and walking together in the night time.

description of May Day 1580 activities in Burnley

Yorkshire takes … nearly every penny of its money but Lancashire takes its water, including that from the sewage works.

Ammon Wrigley (born 1862)
on Saddleworth

She eats her porridge with a wide-mouthed spoon.

Nineteenth-century saying from Rossendale describing a talkative woman

They olluz say'n there's th' most thrutchin' wheer there's th' least reawm.

Edwin Waugh, nineteenth-century dialect writer

Lancashire is often said to have been 'remote from London', as though nearness to London was all that really counted. We, of course, are well aware that it was London which was remote from Lancashire.

Alan Crosby, A History of Lancashire, *1998*

Though many a pleasant nook
In many a land I've seen
I'd wander back to my own green hills
If the wide world lay in between.
They say there's bluer skies
Across the foaming sea,
Each man that is born has a land
of his own
And this is the land for me.

*'Here's to my native land' by Edwin
Waugh, born in Rochdale in 1817*

Weddin's nowt, 'ousekeepin's all.

Lancashire verdict on married life

No-one misses a slice off a cut loaf.

*justification for taking another man's wife
out for immoral purposes, 1920s*

Red cattle standing knee-deep in the blue-flecked river; watermeadows with the plaintive curlew wheeling overhead; lush fields deep in buttercup gold, hedges vivid with red campion, and blue forget-me-nots peeping shyly.

Herbert Collins on the Ribble, 1950

Hodder and Calder and Ribble and rain,
All meet together in Mytton demesne.

There is a great deal of urbanity and polished manners, without any of the affectation of high breeding, and the treatment of strangers here is proverbially hospitable.

Baines on Liverpool, 1825

Here, not one in ten can speak their native language tolerably; not more than one in twenty correctly; and of these last, scarce one tenth can boast any greater literary acquirement than that of their grammar.

Ellen Weeton, from Upholland,
on Liverpool people, 1840

And what shall I say of the Lancashire working-class? That they are the most intelligent of any in the island — in the world … in mechanics they are unsurpassed and probably turn out a greater amount of work than any other equal number of people under the sun. They are ardent in temperament and of honest intention.

Samuel Bamford, Walks in South Lancashire, *1844*

The people here are fully aware of the importance of their labour, and take their reward as a matter of simple right, looking upon any expression of thanks as an unworthy sign of inferiority and dependence.

Richard Ayton, 1813

Eaur Lanky lads an' their gaffers
Has built aw th' bloomin' earth
An' there isn't a job that's wo'th owt
But Lancashire gan it birth.

Allen Clarke, 1923

'We buried 'im wi' 'am.'

a proper Lancashire funeral

Before they reached Milton, they saw a deep lead-coloured cloud hanging on the horizon and near to the town the air had a faint taste and smell of smoke.

Elizabeth Gaskell, North and South, *1854 (Milton was based on Manchester)*

A tourist in Lancashire has to search
for objects of interest, different from
those which excited his attention in
other lands; he has to contemplate
stupendous triumphs of science and
art, instead of the wondrous works
of nature; he has to deal with the
present and the future, scarcely
finding time to bestow inquiry
or reflection on the past.

anonymous, 1843

If I were capable of painting in words the impression Liverpool made on my imagination, it would form a beautiful picture indeed!

Lord Erskine, late eighteenth century

Liverpool is the town of my heart, and I would rather sail a mud-flat there than command a clipper ship out of London.

John Masefield, poet laureate 1930-67

From this ridge there are moments
when the sun breaks through cloud
masses and effulgent silvery rays light
up the surrounding hills.

Herbert Collins, 1950, on Thieveley Pike

When Pendle wears a woolly cap
The farmers all may take a nap,
When Pendle Hill doth wear a hood
Be sure the day will not be good.

Removed from the enervating and seductive temptations of a city, and forced for the most part to earn their bread under the broad canopy of heaven, it is not surprising to find that the people were a long-lived and vigorous race.

Poulton-le-Fylde in the eighteenth century

Manchester. It is not to be called the City Beautiful, though it has beauty. It is not old, though it has links with our medieval days. It is not spectacular like Liverpool, or spacious like Leeds, and it does not stir the imagination as York and Bristol do. And yet it is one of the greatest cities in the world, and one of the most English.

Arthur Mee, 1936

When all England is aloft,
Well are they that are in Christ's Croft
And where should Christ's Croft be?
But between Ribble and Mersey?

We land on the flat shore on the Liverpool side and are contented to ride through the water for some length … on the shoulders of some honest Lancashire clown who comes knee deep to the boat side, to truss you up and then runs away with you.

Daniel Defoe arriving at Liverpool from Birkenhead, 1720

The simple fact is that it is a bewildering county — a county of violent contrasts and amazing diversity ... it is a county of lingering legends and vivid history, of industrial ardour and idyllic repose — contrasts always.

J Cumming Walters, 1929

Take Lancashire and all it stands for from Britain, and at once we become an unimportant storm-bound island lost in the mists of the north.

Walter Greenwood, 1935

Also in this series:

The Little Book of Yorkshire
ISBN 1 85568 194 3

The Little Book of the Lake District
ISBN 1 85568 200 1

The Little Book of Wit & Wisdom
ISBN 1 85568 209 5

For a full list of our books, calendars,
videos, cassettes and magazines,
visit www.dalesman.co.uk